NIGHT

POEMS BY
SULOCHANA MANANDHAR

TRANSLATED BY
MUNA GURUNG

TILTED AXIS PRESS 2019
THANKS TO OUR KICKSTARTER BACKERS

TRANSLATOR'S NOTE

I met Sulo in 2014. Our first meeting took place long-distance when another writer, Manjushree Thapa, sent me ten of Sulo's poems from the collection *Raat* (*Night*) to translate for *Words Without Borders*. Sulo's poems arrived at a time when I was wrestling with my own Nepaliness — what did it mean, I was wondering, to be a Nepali writer writing in English? How was I going to breathe life into my relationship with the Nepali language? Am I Nepali enough?

Sulo's poems provided answers to these questions, but not the ones I could have imagined. Her writing taught me that Nepali literature doesn't have to be difficult or inaccessible in the way I have known it to be. Small and quiet, her poems invited me to sit down, to slow down. They told me that I didn't have to be afraid of them. I took advice from her poem, 'Friend':

Do not complain about darkness, instead
light a light
Do not run away from night, instead
become night's friend

Translating Sulo's work allowed me to befriend the Nepali language again, and it also became a reminder of how I am always enough. Enough of a writer, enough of a translator, enough of a Nepali woman.

—

The poems in this collection were mostly written at night about night. At the beginning, Sulo recalls them as insomniac notes in her diary, written on nights when her heart rattled in pain over what she had seen, heard, endured during the day. Unlike Sulo, I sleep deeply, straight through to morning. Rarely do I find myself restless in the thick hours of night or sleeplessly sifting thoughts. Feeling like an inexperienced insomniac, I set alarms for various odd hours of the night to method-translate some of these poems, but I could barely stay awake!

The good news is that Sulo's poems are built both for the wakeful and the restful. Even in their brevity, her poems are expansive. To me, *Night* is especially about being a woman and finding in darkness a comfort that she is unable to find elsewhere, or in anyone. But Sulo doesn't simply gender night, she refers to night as 'ऊ', which in the Nepali language is the gender non-specific third person pronoun. At the beginning, I found myself accidentally translating night as 'she/her', and in editing saw that not only was it an inaccurate translation but it was also limiting, because in Sulo's poetry, night is a mother, a boatman, a teacher, a friend, a conversation, an idea, a separate time of its own, both specific and shapeless.

In its original form, *Night* is a collection of sixty

poems, but in this incarnation, it has become a chapbook of twenty-five selected pieces. The selections are mine alone, although I have made sure to include Sulo's favourite poem, 'Expecting'. This chapbook isn't Sulo's complete collection, then, but I hope you will receive it as its own separate expression, perhaps a branch of her original work even, and one that reads, I hope, seamlessly as a whole, not as one half of something larger.

As in any translation, I've struggled with the question of 'accuracy' for this project. Should I stay close to the source language and the poems' forms, or should I move freely but stay true to the emotional heart of the poems as they travel from one language to another? Poet and friend, Christina Olivares, would ask me about the 'vibe' of the poems in the original language. 'What's the vibe?' she'd comment in the margins of my translations. That simple question has helped the process of translating Sulo's work. I have chosen to stick closer to the 'vibe' of Sulo's poems, rather than attempt a word-for-word translation. In the editing process, Sophie Collins (who's been incredible!) and I have kept our eyes and ears tuned towards the lives of these poems in this particular iteration: how are they living together in this book?

Addressing that question, we've made some bold and specific decisions. We've taken liberties with changing the titles of many of the poems (you'll find more direct title translations in the Notes section). We did this, partly to avoid repetition (the longer titles of the Nepali seemed to give away much of the poem's content in the English before it had really begun) which felt more careless, or even accidental, than purposeful in the translations. Traditional Nepali poetry recitation aesthetics call for a repetition of the first line and the last lines of poems. We found the repetition in Sulo's poems lived in the titles being slight mirror-images of the first lines. We've preserved this repetition or echo not within a poem but across poems. The titles in this translation have also become shorter, mostly because poems from *Night* have always come to me in a soft, quiet manner, and long titles in the English seemed to detract – visually – from that quiet. Similarly, we have removed all of the exclamation marks (!) that are in Sulo's Nepali texts. If in the Nepali the exclamation mark could connote an echo in its poetic expression, in the English the symbol became simply loud and clashed dramatically with the softness of the poems. We closely studied all the punctuations and have tried to mimic and retain the structure of the poems by leaving trails of ellipses, dashes, commas, and periods in places akin to those in the source poems. We have, though, taken out a lot of punctuation, especially at the end of the poems. The choice of reducing the number of punctuation and shortening the titles was also to give these twenty-five poems a sense of continuity as the reader moves from one poem to another. The entire chapbook is a single poem, broken into many poems, much like Sulo's night is a single night broken into many nights.

—

I am lucky, to say the least, and indebted to Sulo for being the kind of poet who has been incredibly generous and trusting in allowing me to take these liberties. None of this without you, Sulo. Thank you.

Deborah, thank you for choosing us, for being patient and generous with time. Sophie, you're magic; this book looks so good because of you! I'd like to thank a few more people who helped me get to this point: Manjushree, for introducing me to Sulo and her work; Prawin Adhikari, for always pushing me to translate, for being a bridge and making the connections I sometimes miss; everyone who believe in women translating women and literature from Asia, and supported the fundraiser; and lastly, Bhushan, for being my walking-talking Nepali dictionary, for listening to me always, for bringing me closer to this language we share.

Muna Gurung

AUTHOR'S NOTE: NIGHT AND WOMEN

Everyone, in one form or another, has poetic consciousness in them. The only difference is that this consciousness blooms in some, while in others it stays hidden. Women, after all, are the source of creation and are therefore full of poetic consciousness. But often labelled 'Housewife Poems', many of our grandmothers', mothers' and sisters' poetry has been cast to a corner of the kitchen, and usually burned with wood fire or washed away with the stains of baby rags.

When I say this, it's possible that you hear echoes of feminism in my voice. But whether I'm a feminist or not, I can't say. From a young age, the compassion and principles in me seem like they were made to be on the side of social justice, if there is feminism in me, it is the kind of feminism that fits within the confines of social justice and equality.

Like carvings on stone, the injustices of the day etch themselves deeply in the grooves of my mind. They question me throughout the night and rattle my sleep. So, I take night as my guide and my support to find the answers to these questions. Having conversed so frequently with night, it has become a friend, an invaluable teacher and many times, it has been a selfless boatman that has helped me safely cross many rivers of dilemma. Sometimes, my night feels like my own wealth that no one else can claim, and sometimes it feels like my own beloved mother. I have sat in night's lap and jotted down my thoughts and feelings, and some of these have become poems.

Many see night as a symbol of darkness, but I see night as a mother who gives birth to light. I am a woman. There are many who view women as second class citizens, but if women didn't exist, how can a complete world be created? Similarly, there are many who view night solely as a form of darkness. But if night didn't exist, what will a world of endless daylight be like?

These poems that I have scribbled in the night are now translated into the English language and have emerged in front of a larger world. I am excited and grateful to those who have given me their love and support all these years. If Muna Gurung hadn't taken up the project of translating these poems, how could they have reached you? Without publisher, Deborah Smith and her team at Tilted Axis Press, and editor, Sophie Collins, how could the poems be realised in this book form?

I am indebted to all, even to night.

Sulochana

WINGS

Softly, night arrives
gives me wings, and leaves

I wear them
out into a world
I've created

roaming any which way

BIRTH

Knowledge was born from night's womb
and from the same womb
came light

Unknowable night
stretching into darkness,

what else
are you trying to bring to life?

PROPERTY

Night –
my ancestral inheritance, my birthright

Shall I cover myself with it or lie on it?
Shall I look upon it as a mirror or a field?
Shall I keep it in my heart or scatter it?
Shall I surrender to night's embrace
or play with it until I'm sated?

My night is no one's property
is the land in which I feel free
where I no longer fear subjugation

MOTHER

When I fall into
night's arms, its lap
I become fearless

night becomes my mother

how beloved
how warm

SLEEP (1)

I want to dream a new dream

DISAPPEARANCE

Does day fade into night
or does night fade into day?

Time chews
time swallows
this large chatāmari bread –
a blend of night and day

Silently, I watch
the chatāmari slowly disappear
I, too, am slowly disappearing

MOON

How dark –
the moon, the fireflies
are missing tonight

This night is deep, thick
the heart's voice
is missing tonight

How stifling –
this endless darkness
The moon, the fireflies are missing tonight

BOAT

Rowing his heavy boat
along the edges of time
the old fisherman dutifully
ferries travellers across the river,
wasting a little with every journey

Like the fisherman, night
delivers me
to the banks of morning

Waking, I open the doors of my heart
see the whole world waiting for me
I take joy in that world
I get lost in it,
forgetting night, just as the travellers
forget the fisherman and his boat…

FRIEND

Do not complain about darkness, instead
light a light
Do not run away from night, instead
become night's friend

STRANGE PICTURE

Outside, dark
inside, bright
Moles like hills
hills like moles
Illusion like truth
truth like illusion…

Night
is an unfathomable picture –

what kind of artist
could dream up such a thing?

SHADOW

Night becomes Time
keeps me company
becomes shapeless
to give me shape

Night is my shadow
and my reflection
a reminder of my true form

When night fades into day
where will I see myself?

PAIN

Night endures
chronic pain

How much longer must it suffer?
Who will break the news?

Night has always endured
this disease –
silently,
alone

as though receiving punishment
for the mistakes
humans have made

JOURNEY

Difficult journey
night's journey
Lonely journey
night's journey

On dangerous roads
of memories or dreams
when the heart stumbles, lacerated
at the bend
of the cliff
there is no hand to reach out for
and if the wounded heart were to cry through
 the night
no one would hear

Night is a jungle
the journey through which
can only be taken alone

RICH SOIL

Night – rich soil of silence
where I sow exquisite dreams,
harvest pleasure,
filling the granary

How beautiful night is!
A country of infinite dreams

DISTINCTIONS

Divided into segments
One night can feel like many

In sleep
in dreams
in restless, wakeful thoughts
night reveals itself in distinct forms

Sometimes night is a Swarna Yug,
sometimes a Kali Yug

SLEEP (2)

If night doesn't want to sleep, instead
treat it like day

Receive it as a gift,
an extension of day's lifespan
Watch it silently meld into the soft light of dawn
—

by then, even if you've come to desire night
it won't stay with you

DISORDER

At midnight
the neighbourhood is drunk with sleep
An unfathomable quiet…

There's not a sound outside and yet
disorder seeps through
rises like steam
a voice with no sound

Where does it come from?

KINGDOM OF DOGS

Night has spread
into darkness.
Dogs continue barking

Is this not a kingdom of dogs?
I ask. I touch myself
It seems I still have a human heartbeat
inside me

PROTEST

Night rolls further and further
away — a wave

I try to draw it back
to keep it within reach
but it resists
breaks onto shore

Night is protesting —
is it calling for morning?

EXPECTING

Night is an expectant mother
If you are doubtful, just wait;
early tomorrow morning
it will give birth to the sun

SIEVE

I pour scattered pieces of my heart
on night's sieve
and begin to sift

The countless worries of my heart
one by one become distinct –
grains of envy and discomfort

I sift all night
alone
hoping that, at the very least
this act will purify
my offering to morning

CONVERSATION

Night is lonely
in this quiet
and I am lonely too

Our silent conversation
washes the dirt
from our hearts

Night is moving towards the light
and I, too, am brightening

QUEEN

Why is she who blooms bold at night
so afraid of the day?

Queen of Night –
I would become night
to see her beauty,
a glimpse of her being

I would become dark to witness her beauty

GURU

At midnight
night itself
comes to me as a guardian, wakes me
becomes a guru
teaching me life

When I try to express my gratitude
night becomes invisible, melts –
silence into silence

WAKING

I was in a deep sleep,
but even in its silence
night woke me

Afterwards, a flickering of lights

NOTES ON THE TRANSLATIONS

'Disappearance', p. 10: chatāmari is a thin rice crepe, a Newari specialty.

'Distinctions', p. 19: according to Hinduism, the world undergoes four stages or eras called yugs or yugas. Kali Yug is the final stage and the stage that the world is thought to currently be in. It is a time where humans are furthest away from god, where there is greed, destruction, malcontent. Swarna Yug is a stage of Sulo's own invention; it is a time when everything is golden, heavenly and beautiful.

'Sieve', p. 25: nanglo is the Nepali word that

is used in the source poem and that we have replaced here with 'sieve' in order to better serve the cadence of the English-language translation. A nanglo is a winnowing tray.

Alternative titles for the translations in this pamphlet are, consecutively, as follows: 'Night's Wings', 'Mysterious Night', 'To Dream a New Dream', 'Descent', 'Night of the Missing Moon', 'Old Fisherman', 'Lonely Journey', 'A Country of Dreams', 'Divided Night', 'If Night Doesn't Want to Sleep', 'Silent Neighbourhood', 'Night's Protest', 'Pregnant Night', 'On Night's Winnowing Tray', 'Silent Conversation', 'Queen of the Night' and 'After Waking'.

Yeoyu— new voices Korea

Eight exquisitely designed & highly collectible chapbooks with enthralling new short stories from:

Han Kang	tr. Deborah Smith
Cheon Heerahn	tr. Emily Yae Won
Han Yujoo	tr. Janet Min
Bae Suah	tr. Deborah Smith
Jeon Sung-tae	tr. Sora Kim-Russell
Hwang Jeung-eun	tr. Jeon Seung-hee
Kang Hwa Gil	tr. Mattho Mandersloot
Kim Soom	tr. Emily Yae Won

www.strangers.press/yeoyu £35

Copyright
© Sulochana Manandhar 2019
Translations copyright © Muna Gurung 2019

This edition published in the United Kingdom by Tilted Axis Press in 2019. This translation was funded by Arts Council England and 278 brilliant Kickstarter backers. Thank you!

tiltedaxispress.com

The right of Sulochana Manandhar to be identified as the author of these works, and that of Muna Gurung as the translator, have been asserted in accordance with Section 77 of the Copyright, Designs and Patent Act 1988.

This is a work of fiction. Names, characters, places and incidents are either the product of the author's imagination or are used fictitiously. Any resemblance to any actual persons, living or dead, events or locales is entirely coincidental.

ISBN (chapbook)   9781911284246
ISBN (ebook)   9781911284345

A catalogue record for this book is available from the British Library.

Edited by Sophie Collins
Cover design by Soraya Gilanni Viljoen
Typesetting and ebook production by Simon Collinson
Printed and bound by Footprint Workers Co-op, Leeds